follow your heart

everyday wisdom for an extraordinary life

BIG SKY PUBLISHING
www.bigskypublishing.com.au

Illustrations and words by josh langley

Big Sky Publishing Pty Ltd
PO Box 303, Newport, NSW 2106, Australia
Phone: 1300 364 611
Fax: (61 2) 9918 2396
Email: info@bigskypublishing.com.au
Web: www.bigskypublishing.com.au

Cover design and typesetting: Think Productions

Printed in China through Asia Pacific Offset Limited

National Library of Australia Cataloguing-in-Publication entry (pbk)
Author: Langley, Josh.
Title: Follow your heart : everyday wisdom for an extraordinary life / Josh Langley.
ISBN: 9781922132062 (pbk.)
Series: Langley, Josh. Frog & the well.
Subjects: Happiness--Quotations, maxims, etc.
              Inspiration--Quotations, maxims, etc.
              Happiness--Popular works.
Dewey Number: 158.1

National Library of Australia Cataloguing-in-Publication entry
Author: Langley, Josh.
Title: Follow your heart [electronic resource] : everyday wisdom for an extraordinary life / Josh Langley.
ISBN: 9781922132079 (ebook)
Series: Langley, Josh. Frog & the well.
Subjects: Happiness--Quotations, maxims, etc.
              Inspiration--Quotations, maxims, etc.
Dewey Number: 158.1

follow your heart

Your heart is trying to tell you something.

That small little voice inside has something important to say. It's time to listen.

To the time poor, the over worked, the stressed,
the ridiculed, the laughed at, the lovers, the dreamers,
and the child in all of us – this book is for you.

Thanks to two awesome sisters Diane and Sharon for
believing in a little frog and a beautiful lady called Val
who started me on this crazy adventure.

follow your heart

Introduction: head or the heart?

We're so distracted leading crazy, busy lives that we forget to listen to our heart and follow our passion. Sometimes, we're too scared to follow something that could take us out of our comfort zone and make us face change head on.

Since an early age, we've been conditioned to be logical, be rational, think things through, play it safe and play by the rules. But your heart doesn't care for rules, it's the wild, loving, passionate, adventurous part

of you that wants to express itself, to be free and do things because they feel right.

When we learn to listen to our heart and bravely follow it, our level of happiness increases by a million times. Not because life becomes easier, but because life becomes more exciting, more tasty, more colourful, more fun and more 'you'.

Here's some everyday wisdom for an extraordinary life.

Love bravely

Our head thinks our heart needs protection, when
in fact our heart can handle anything thrown at it.
Your heart wants to experience everything;
it wants to love wildly without holding back.

So we have to be brave and trust
our heart knows what it's doing.

Be kind to yourself, you're worth it.

Everyone is beautiful,
in their own unique way.

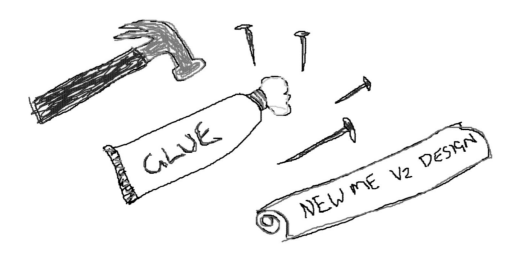

Don't panic, you're not broken, you're just being remodelled into something more awesome!

You are perfect in a beautifully imperfect way.

Embrace your strangeness,
it's what makes you so adorable.

No matter how bad you feel, things will get better.

No matter how bad things get,
there will always be rainy day friends.

You're never really alone.

As long as you can manage a smile, that's enough to get you through even the crappiest of days.

A broken heart is never really the end;
it could be the beginning of something amazing.

When you're feeling down,
    Mother Nature will always help pick you up again.

Everyone goes through an awkward stage,

even supermodels.

Love all parts of your body,
including your bum!

The most important person in the world for you to love … is you.

So keep saying nice things to yourself.

Trust yourself; you're wiser than you think.

Ladybirds can fly too, what's your hidden talent?

Think differently

If you keep doing the same thing over and over and expect a different result then you must be mad.

So instead of thinking with your head all the time, think with your heart and you'll be closer to where you really want to be.

So ask yourself, 'what would my heart do?'

Dare to dream BIG!

Life's too short to worry about wrinkles;
                    just go to the beach and enjoy yourself.

Be eccentric if you want to.

Don't worry about what others think of you;
just believe in your own fabulousness.

Share your story, it might just inspire others.

Surprise someone with kindness.

You may not know where you're going,
but it's where you're meant to be.

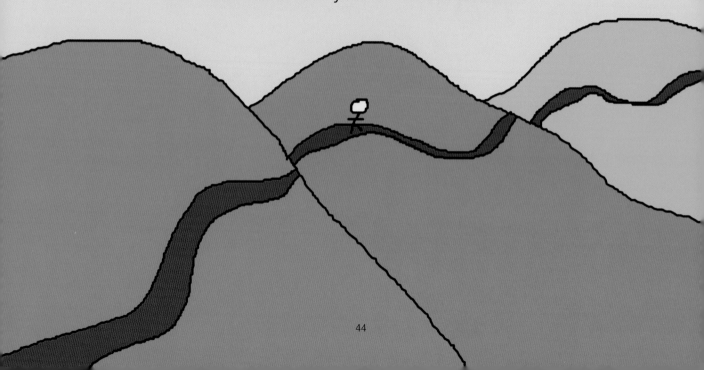

Think abundance.
You've always got more to be grateful for than you think.

Love people for who they are and they'll love you for who you are.

Love doesn't judge anyone,
     so don't let anyone judge your love.

If you try to understand people before judging them
you can avoid all sorts of crazy misunderstandings.

Some things aren't worth getting your knickers in a knot about; just let it go.

Love the planet like you would a good friend.

Don't keep up with the Joneses,
  they've got no idea what's going on either.

Treat those aches and pains as a good sign
you're not dead yet.

A kind gesture to someone today,
will come back to you later when you most need it.

Spend quality time with yourself.

It does seem that as we get older,
the path of life needs more toilet stops.

Find joy in the simple and silly things.

Let the randomness of life surprise you.

Trust life to know where its going.

When was the last time you flew a kite?

When you do something,
　　　don't hold back,
　　　　　give your best.

When you're happy, show it!

Feeling good is extremely infectious.

Follow your heart,
   who knows what kind of adventures you'll have!

Live fully

We don't want to look back at our lives and wish we'd done this or done that, gone skydiving, said you're sorry, taken that holiday to the Bahamas, travelled to the moon and learned to paint like Picasso.

Now is the time to put aside your scared, way too logical mind and really squeeze the most out of this life.

Go for it.

Express yourself in the best way you know how.

Lie back on the grass and watch the clouds and feel all your stress and worry just float away.

Always expect to find something wonderful
just around the corner.

Relish those quiet times when it's just you and big cup of coffee.

Sneak afternoon naps wherever you can,
you'll feel better for it.

If you really want to believe in fairies,
then go ahead – it's your reality!

Exercise your freewill,
　　　give work a miss and go on a picnic instead.

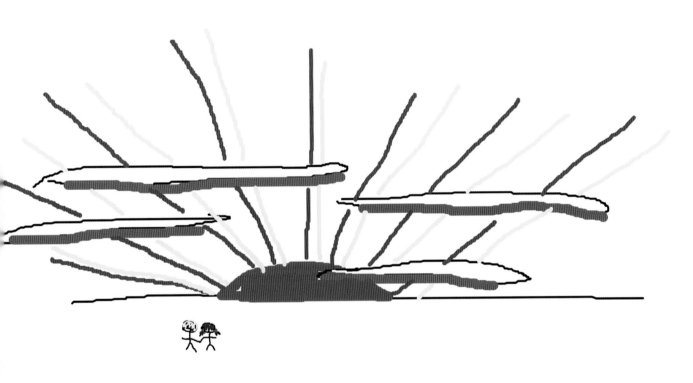

Watch sunsets with someone you love.

Plant a veggie garden.
Home grown tastes way better.

If the kids can get dirty in the garden, then so can you!

Never rush a hug.

Read a poem to a tree.

Hug a rainbow.

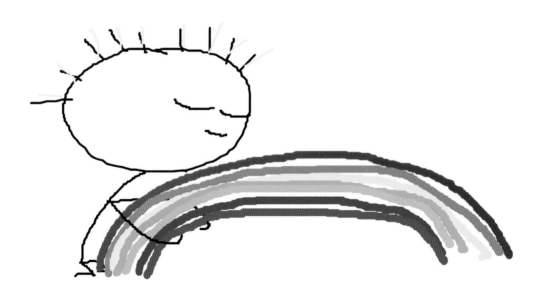

Collect more experiences than 'things'.

Take a different route to … anywhere.

Never stop believing in magic,
world peace and unicorns called Bernard.

Make time to daydream.

Watch less TV.

Run through the backyard naked.

Touch someone's heart.

Dance like a free range chicken.

Be amazed by the beauty of Mother Nature.

Live your life in your own unique way.

Let go of grudges – you'll feel much happier.

Unleash your imagination,
    you'll be amazed at what you can create.

Don't take yourself too seriously.

Be curious about everything, go exploring.

Don't say 'yes', when you really want to say 'no'.
Remember this is your life.

Be fearless, brave, kind and loving all at the same time.

Spend more time relaxing and make space
for those quiet moments of inspiration.

Move, run, walk, dance, jiggle, wiggle, strut, hop, skip, or just wave your hands in the air like you just don't care.

Remember life on earth is one great big adventure;
there's no right or wrong way to do things, just lessons
to be learned.

Let go of being in control
and go with the flow of life.

Always do things that make your soul
sing and your heart shine.

Feel with your heart.
Think with your heart.
Love with your heart.

You can then use your head to count your blessings.

About Frog and the Well

Some stories are strange and others are just out right unexplainable. So for the sake of a good story I'll try and unravel how the idea of the 'Frog' started, even though it borders on the bizarre.

As part of research for another book I was writing, I underwent a past life regression. While I wasn't an American Indian or Cleopatra, I had an experience that sort of shifted something in me. A couple of months after the session I started to draw stick figures and put little inspiring words and phrases to them. The stick figures seemed to have a life of their own and would only come out and play when 'they' wanted to.

I really wanted to share them with the world, but I needed to create a name or theme for the stick figure concept and suddenly 'Frog and the Well' jumped up. Based on the 'Frog in a Well' Tibetan fable which urges us to challenge our way of limited thinking, the title was perfect and the 'Frog' was born.

The Frog's first book *Unconventional Happiness*, was released in November 2011 (exactly 1 year after the first cartoon was created) and *Follow Your Heart* is the next delightful leap in the Frog adventure.

A poet, dreamer, lover of life and gallant explorer, the Frog is an aspect of all of us; he's the little inner child wanting to come out and play.

Continue the journey with the Frog at www.frogandthewell.com

Happy travels,

Josh.